T0131639

# ALL OCCASION
## INSPIRATIONAL POEMS OF
# REALITY

**AUDREY M. VIRGES**

authorHOUSE®

*AuthorHouse™*
*1663 Liberty Drive*
*Bloomington, IN 47403*
*www.authorhouse.com*
*Phone: 1 (800) 839-8640*

*Published by AuthorHouse  04/30/2020*

*ISBN: 978-1-7283-5162-9 (sc)*
*ISBN: 978-1-7283-5160-5 (hc)*
*ISBN: 978-1-7283-5161-2 (e)*

*Library of Congress Control Number: 2020905320*

*Print information available on the last page.*

# Acknowledgements

I thank God for giving me the gift of writing Inspirational poetry. Thanks to my family for their love and support. Thanks to those who have been an inspiration to me, and thanks to my church family and friends for their encouragements.

Thanks to President Barack Obama & Michelle for sending me a card of thanks for my first book LIVING REALITY.

# Contents

# (NEW YEARS POEMS)

# A New Year Has Arrived

A new year has arrived again
Special wishes for you my dear,
I wish you all the happiness there is
And lots, and lots of cheer.

Last year for you was a challenge
I can't say this year won't be the same,
But I do know that if you keep the faith
You'll keep calling on Jesus' name.

So just you embrace this new beginning
Start everything fresh and new.
May you have a wonderful, and rewarding year
And may all your New Year dreams come true.

Audrey M. Virges

# Happy New Year

Wishing you a Happy New Year
For you I express my love,
You can say farewell to last year
You're blessed to see this year from above.

There are so many things I want to do
And for this year it's the beginning,
Let me share this year with you
And we'll hope for a happy ending.

Lets gear up and get this year on the roll
You have many aspirations to betide,
Hang tough, and give it your all
Get ready to enjoy the ride.

Audrey M. Virges

# (VALENTINE POEMS)

# My Valentine

You were my Valentine since the day we met
And the years have gone by fast,
We have been married twenty years
And I prayed our love would last,

While we were rearing our children
And managing our home,
Many obstacles came our way,
But no matter what obstacles we faced
You were my Valentine to stay.

God has blessed us so many years
And our love is still going strong,
I know we are meant for each other
And with each other we belong.

You were my Valentine since the day we met
I love you more now than then,
I'll love you always and forever
Even until the end

*Audrey M. Virges*

# My Love Forever

My darling my love we dated two years
And the next year you became my wife,
You have been my Valentine since that day
You bring so much happiness to my life.

Your smile is so radiant
It brings joy from my head to my feet,
When you became my wife
My life was made complete.

You will always be my Valentine
Because you were meant for me,
And you will be my love forever
Throughout eternity.

Audrey M. Virges

# Let's Celebrate Valentine's Day

My precious, my love, my sweetheart sweet
You are the apple of my eye,
You've been my friend since 5th grade
And my Valentine since jr. high.

Since that time our love has grown
I'm looking forward to sharing my life with you,
You are the only one for me
And I hope you feel the same way too.

So let's celebrate this Valentine's day
With the love for each other we share,
Let's celebrate this Valentines day
Showing each other how much we care.

*Audrey M. Virges*

# Be Mine

Will you be my Valentine
And hold my hand real tight?
Will you take a walk with me
And enjoy the beautiful sight?

Will you come and dance with me
With the music sounding so mellow?
Will you sit with me in the park
And watch the sun so yellow?

Will you be my Valentine
And share your life with me?
And we will be in love forever
As happy as can be.

*Audrey M. Virges*

# Valentine's Gifts

A box of candy and a beautiful rose
I give to you today,
To show you that I love you
In a very special way.

You won my heart and blew my mind
So you I can't live without,
You really are my Valentine
I know that without a doubt.

Please accept these gifts as a token of my love
And wrap your arms around my heart,
I love you now, and I'll love you tomorrow
You were my Valentine from the start.

Audrey M. Virges

# You Are My Gift

Thank you honey, for the Valentine roses
They are beautiful and have a beautiful smell,
They really say you love me
From your actions I can tell.

I thank you for the box of candy
With every row layered so neat,
Some days I have a sweet tooth
Now I have lots of candy to eat.

Thank you for taking me out to dinner
And really showing me a good time,
The steaks were delicious, and the dessert was divine.
The restaurant was really a nice place to dine.

I thank you for all the Valentine gifts
And the things you do for me all year through,
But most of all I thank you graciously
For giving me the gift of you.

*Audrey M. Virges*

# My Sweetheart

I want you to be my Sweetheart
And in my future I want you to be,
I have searched, and searched, and searched
And I know you're the one for me.

Please accept me for who I am
And accept me for my past,
My desire is for us to have an honest relationship
Because I want our love to last.

Our life together is waiting for us
Will you be my valentine?
I am excited about our relationship
It's our time to shine.

Audrey M. Virges

# (EASTER POEMS)

# It Was Not The End

Death on the cross
Was a terrible death,
But Jesus hung there
Until His very last breath.
Out of all of His followers
Only a few came to weep,
His mother Mary and a few others
Kneeled at Jesus feet.
A darkness fell on Jerusalem
His body tired, and weary was he,
He cried to His Father in Heaven
Why have You forsaken me?
He hung there quietly suffering
And stayed there for a long period,
And finally He uttered His last words
Father unto You I commend my spirit.
He hung, bled, suffered, and died
But surely that was not the end,
Because on that third day morning
He rose with all power in His hands.

*Audrey M. Virges*

# Easter Day

We put on our new apparel
And off to church we go,
O yes it's Easter Sunday
We'll see people dressed from head to toe.

Children recite their Easter poems
Looking so beautifully adorned,
They tell how our Savior died
And that He rose on Easter morning.

He rose with the greatest purpose
Back to His Father He went,
He fulfilled His mission here on earth
For His time on earth was awesomely spent.

*Audrey M. Virges*

# Jesus Suffered

Our Savior was crucified on the cross
He suffered for you and me,
He could have called ten thousand angels
But He died so our souls would be free.

He died on the cross so willingly
He suffered from all His wounds,
He had to do His Father's will
Afterwards He was laid in the tomb.

An angel came from Heaven
And rolled the stone away,
To find that our Savior had risen
On that precious Easter day.

Audrey M. Virges

# Falsely Accused

Jesus was so sadly falsely accused
He stumbled with the cross on His way to Calvary Hill,
He was hung, stretched, and whipped
By His stripes we are healed.

They whipped 39 stripes on His back
And nailed His hands and feet to the cross,
They speared Him in the side
And placed a crown of 72 thorns on His head
He suffered so we wouldn't be lost.

He cried Father let this cup pass from Me
But it was not His Father's will
Jesus willingly died for us
Out on Calvary Hill.

Audrey M. Virges

# The Dogwood

When Jesus walked the earth
Dogwoods grew big and tall,
The wood could be cut to make anything
And surely it would not fall.

How sadly amazing was it used
To build the cross where upon Jesus would hang,
It is a true reflection
Of Jesus's suffering and pain.

The Dogwood's petals are shaped like a cross
The middle of the flower is shaped like a crown of thorns,
The tip of the petals bear a nail indent
And there are colors in the petals resembling
Jesus's blood that ran down His body on Easter morning.

The tree now grows small, bent, and twisted
And can never be used for a cruel intent again,
But it still reflects Jesus's suffering
At Easter time wherever it stands.

Audrey M. Virges

# Easter Enjoyment

Easter is a fun time to do different things
To add to the holiday excitement,
Buying candy, and making cupcakes
Is a really great deal of delightment.

Children are excited about Easter time
Because their Easter baskets their parents will buy,
And they will get new hair do's and hair cuts
As well as new dresses, pants, shoes, shirts, and ties.

They say their Easter speeches
While looking forward to Easter dinner,
After the egg hunt is over
The Easter meal is a winner.

Easter is a very enjoyable holiday
People visit their families from all directions,
They have fun and enjoy themselves greatly
Remembering that it's about Jesus's
death burial and resurrection.

Audrey M. Virges

# That Glorious Easter Day

I say my Easter poem
Because I am so proud you see,
That Jesus rose on Easter morning
He rose for you and me.

The grave couldn't hold Him
Because there He wasn't supposed to stay,
He ascended back to God His Father
On that glorious Easter day.

Audrey M. Virges

# Church On Easter Morning

We go to church on Easter Morning
To glorify God and to lift Jesus name,
Even though Jesus died for us willingly
He experienced lots of suffering, and pain.

God knew we needed a Savior
Who we can tell our troubles to,
He sent His son Jesus to die for us
And He rose for me and you.

Audrey M. Virges

# Jesus Did His Father's Will

It's great to know about Jesus birth
But there's a lot more to unfold,
He walked the earth and did His Father's will
And that's not all it is to be told.

He completed His mission on earth
But He reign from the time He was born,
Jesus did His best for mankind
When He died for us and rose on Easter morning.

Audrey M. Virges

# Fun Easter

I love Easter day
It's a fun day for me,
I say my speech, and find the eggs
That was hidden behind the tree.

Audrey M. Virges

# Easter Morning

I look forward to Easter morning
To wear my Easter clothes,
And I'm glad to recite my poem to you
That Jesus did and He rose.

Audrey M. Virges

# (MOTHER'S DAY POEMS)

# Mom Is Sweeter

Mom, you're the sweetest person I know
Sweeter than candy and sugar from the grocery store,
Sweeter that syrup that's ready to pour,
Sweeter than a melon pulled from the vine
Sweeter than grapes that make grape wine,
Sweeter than a peach from the orchards down south,
Sweeter than a strawberry placed in your mouth,
Sweeter than apples from an apple tree,
Sweeter than honey from the Honey Bee.
Mom, that's how sweet you are to me.
Happy Mother's Day, Mom.

Audrey M. Virges

# The Model Mother

Happy Mother's Day, Mom
You are truly the meaning of love,
You show us what the joy of being a mom brings
You are a mother sent from above.

You helped us take our first steps
And you nurtured us along the way,
You taught us and helped us shape our lives
As you reared us day by day.

You compliment us when we do good
You hold us when we are sad,
You tried to protect us in every way
And you spanked us when we were bad.

We wish to be like you someday
And repeat the things you've done,
You are the model, Mom
That we wish to become.

Audrey M. Virges

# Mother, You're Special

Mom, you are so special
You do so much for us,
You cook, you clean, you wash and iron
And you rarely ever fuss.

You teach us to do our chores
So lazy we will not be,
You help us with our homework
So good grades we will see.

You teach us to be strong in life
Because one day we will be grown,
You teach us to have good values
So we will live a good life on our own.

Mom, you do so much for us
And you encourage us along the way,
We love and appreciate you, dear Mother Each and every day.
Happy Mother's Day

Audrey M. Virges

# A Mother's Supportive Love

My mother has a special love
That warms my heart each day,
She's so caring, supportive and compassionate
And she prays for me each day.

She listens to my problems
And she wipes away my tears,
She is such an inspiration to me
Just seeing her brings a ray of cheer.

I'm so proud to have a mom like you
You mean the world to me,
So have the happiest Mother's Day
That a mother's day can be.

Audrey M. Virges

# Mom Is the Heart of the Family

Happy Mother's Day, Mom
Just wanted to say again that I love you,
You give such a great meaning to living
And I appreciate everything you do.

You are the heart of the family
And you keep everything rolling along,
You give me good advice to help me live my best
And you always teach me to be strong.

Mom, I love, and adore you
I thank you for teaching me the way,
May God bless you forever, and ever
Have a happy Mother's day.

*Audrey M. Virges*

# My Everything Mom

Happy Mother's Day, Mom
You are an all around everything mom
There's nothing you don't do,
You tend to our family excellent
And we love everything you do.

You are a sweet loving mother with an awesome look
And not only that, you are a very good cook.
You are a housekeeper and a floor sweeper,
You are a pie maker and a cake baker,
You are a good clothes and wound mender,
And you are an awesome baby tender,
You are a nose cleaner and a bottle weaner,
You are a floor mopper and a popcorn popper,
You are a grocery buyer and a shoe tyer,
You are a yard raker and a jelly maker.

Mom, you are all these things and more.
Happy Mother's Day

Audrey M. Virges

# A Mother's Hug

A hug from you, Mom, means so much
It gives my day a wonderful start,
It seems as though there's magic in your hug
Because it's the language of your heart.

Mom, your hugs bond us together
It lets me know you love me so dear,
It makes me feel really secure
And it helps me feel less fear.

I love getting hugs from you, Mom
They give me warmth and make my day,
You show me you're proud to be my mom
Love and affection go a long way.
Happy Mother's Day

Audrey M. Virges

# An Unfailing Love

Mom, you gave the gift of life to me
Your hands held me, and you kissed my little face,
You have been there for me from day one
I got attached quickly to your warm embrace.

You held me in your arms when I had a bad dream
You sang me to sleep when I had a restless night.
You read stories to me when I was board
You love me so much; you spoiled me just right.

You walked me on top of your feet
You raced with me and let me win,
Later you taught me how to cook and study well
Because soon college would be just around the bend.

You coached me until I could make it on my own
And for you, Mom, I thank God above,
You taught me well, and I'll pattern my life after you
Thank you Mom, for having an unfailing love.

Audrey M. Virges

# Mom, My Flower

Dear Mom, I love you so much
More than the world will ever know,
You're my beautiful flower
With each petal so fine,
You are my flower
Full of sunshine.
Happy Mother's Day

Audrey M. Virges

# Mom, You're My Heart

Mom, you are my heart
You mean everything to me,
I am proud to be your daughter
You love me unconditionally.

Your hands are warm and tender
Your arms they hold me tight,
You are such a loving, and caring person
I love you with all my might.
Happy Mother's Day

Audrey M. Virges

# I'm Proud You're Mine

A mother's love is wonderful
A mother's love really shines,
I am proud to stand here today
And say how proud I am you're mine.
Happy Mother's Day

*Audrey M. Virges*

# I'll Love You Forever

To my mom on Mother's Day
You're my life; you're my all,
You have a great love for me
And you really stand tall.

I love you now and I'll love you forever
I love you in every way,
I love you all year long
Not just on Mother's Day
Happy Mother's Day

Audrey M. Virges

# The Best Mom

Hi Mom, you're the best
At everything you do,
You wipe my tears
You hold me tight
You kiss me when I'm feeling blue.
No love could take the place
Of my love I have for you.
Happy Mother's Day

*Audrey M. Virges*

# My Love For You

Happy Mother's Day, Mom
I'm just a little lad
But I can say to you today,
That I love you dearly
On this Happy Mother's Day

Audrey M. Virges

**R.I.P**
★ ★ ★

# (MEMORIAL POEMS)

# I Think of You

I think of you when I rise
Each day that I awake,
I think of the times we shared together
And the memories that we made.

It pleases me to know you left in peace
And all is well with your soul,
You were always quiet and humble
And you really had a heart of gold.

I'll keep your memory in my heart
No matter where I go or what I do,
You gave me such a strong part of you
That I know I can make it through.

Even though I miss you dearly
Your memory will never fade,
Every time I think of you
I'll think of the memories that we made.

*Audrey M. Virges*

# We Will Meet Again

We cherish the life we shared with you
It seemed to have ended too quick,
But God knew when to call you home
A beautiful flower He did pick.

You were an asset to our family
And to our church family as well,
You were friendly to everyone you met
A christian you were everyone could tell.

We will greatly miss your presence
And sometimes I know we'll cry,
But one day we will meet again
In the sweet bye and bye.

Audrey M. Virges

# Your Memory Will Live On

My heart is heavy because you're gone
But I knew you could not stay,
God whispered come on home my child
And to Heaven you made your way.

Now I cannot talk with you
And your hands I cannot touch,
I remembered the wonderful times we had
I love you very much.

You always had a sunny disposition
You made so many people smile,
You had compassion on those in need
And for your family you would go the last mile.

Only time will ease the pain of losing you
But I'm glad you're in your heavenly home,
I love and cherish the times we shared
Because your memory will always live on.

*Audrey M. Virges*

# In God's Care

Your journey was completed
You had nothing else to do,
It was time for you to meet your maker
With a glorified body all new.

You kept the world laughing
You were the center of attention too,
You were also the life of the party
We hated so much to lose you.

God has you now in His mansion above
And you are safe in His care,
When God calls, and it's our time to answer
We will meet you up there.

Audrey M. Virges

# (FATHER'S DAY POEMS)

# My Dad

Dad, I really love and appreciate you
And I notice all the things you do,
You take care of the responsibilities of our home
And you take care of Mom and us too.

You work every day to pay the bills
And you manage to do other chores at home,
You take out the trash and wash the cars
And on weekends you mow the lawn.

You make sure we have proper recreation
You take us to the movies, and we go on picnics and such,
Most importantly you care about our spiritual life
So you take our family to church.

Dad, you're a great influence in my life
You have reared me from a lad,
I look up to you, I salute you, I love you
I'm so proud you're my dad.

Audrey M. Virges

# Dad Gives of Himself

Happy Father's Day, Dad
I love you from my heart so dear,
Just wanted you to know
I appreciate you all through the year.

You are my pillar of strength
And for me I know you know what's best,
You work hard to support our family
And you get very little rest.

I thank you for the things you buy for us
Even though we're not a family of wealth,
One thing I appreciate the most
The time you give of yourself.

*Audrey M. Virges*

# Dad, You're the Best

Happy Father's Day, Dad, you're the best
I am as proud of you as I can be,
I want you to know that I believe in you
And I'm proud you believe in me.

I adore the way you protect our family
And how you try hard to make ends meet,
And how you spend money buying our clothes
So we can look presentable from our head to our feet.

You love to show us off; you're so proud of us.
You stand by us come what may,
You provide for us excellent
As you face the issues of life day by day.

Thank you, Dad, for being there for us
You're the best dad in the world,
You are my shining star
Because Dad, I'm your little girl.

*Audrey M. Virges*

# A Supportive Dad

Dad, you're the strong man in my life
since the time I rode on your shoulder,
Now I'm driving my own car
And I've grown to be much older.

You supported the things that I was interested in
When I needed to talk to you I made a call,
When I needed your help
You caught me as I began to fall.

You support me when I play sports
And you set up my activity fund,
So many things you have done for me
And you wanted nothing in return.

I love you, Dad, for your guidance and support
All integrated with lots of fun,
I appreciate you so much, Dad
And I am grateful to be your son.
Happy Father's Day

*Audrey M. Virges*

# A True Dad

Dad, you have an unconditional love
That can never be replaced,
And you express this love for all your children
No matter what family issues you may face.

You bring out the best in us
You have given us a wonderful life,
You show us what a true man is
The way you respect us, our mom; your wife.

Dad, you taught us to love and be kind to others
You believed that the golden rule is the key,
You're wonderful and I wish to follow in your footsteps
Because you live the way you want us to be.
Happy Father's Day

Audrey M. Virges

# Dad and I Have Fun Together

I love you Dad, because we do fun things together
It's things we do in different kinds of weather.
You take me on picnics on sunny days
And we eat every delicious bite,
When the wind begin to blow
You take me out to fly my kite.
On beautiful days we would go on a hike
And if we weren't tired we would ride our bikes.
When it was raining outside
Like it would sometimes be,
I would play my playstation games
And dad would look at T. V.
Thank you Dad, for the fun things we do
Thank you Dad; I love you.

Audrey M. Virges

# Dad

Happy Father's Day, Dad, you are a very sporty guy
And you are as cool as a cucumber too,
You are an inspiration to me
May all your wishes and dreams come true.

You tell me how important I am to you
And you are important to me too,
For as long as I live
I wish abundant blessings for you.

*Audrey M. Virges*

# My Dad Is Great

Hi Dad, you're the best
You're the best in every way,
I'll love you for the rest of my life
Happy Father's Day

Audrey M. Virges

# Our Dad

To our dad who is there for us
You are the meaning of love,
You are truly a loving dad
Sent from above.
Happy Father's Day

*Audrey M. Virges*

# Dad Does ManyThings

Dad, you wears many hats
And my hat is off to you,
You're so special to our family
You truly love us and we truly love you.
Happy Father's Day

*Audrey M. Virges*

# (BIRTHDAY POEMS)

# Birthday Wishes

This is a very special day
Your birthday has come again,
You have a cake on the table, and gifts all wrapped
And balloons in your hand.

As you blow out the candles
Think how blessed you are,
To be surrounded by friends and family
You're more than blessed by far.

Birthdays only come once a year
And I wish the best for you,
So eat your cake, and open your gifts
And may all your birthday wishes and dreams come true.

Audrey M. Virges

# Happy Birthday, My Baby Boy

It's your birthday, Son
And it's time for the party to begin,
We're here at your favorite skating rink
With all your family and friends.

You have many things to play on
There's bouncy houses to jump in and crawl through,
You have a ping pong table to play on
A floor in which to skate, and other games too.

The pizza has been ordered
On the table are chips and dip
There are meatballs, and chicken salad
And even a few rib tips.

Happy Birthday to you, Son
May you enjoy this day so grand
Happy birthday to our baby boy
Mom and Dad's little man.

*Audrey M. Virges*

# My Friend's Birthday

To my best friend on your birthday
I wish only the best for you,
You are honest, reliable, and very supportive
May all your birthday wishes come true.

You are such a wonderful person
You're there for me come what may,
I wish you all the joy and happiness
That you birthday brings today.

Read your cards, and open your gifts
And be blessed with happiness and cheer,
I wish for you a happy birthday
That will last from year to year.

*Audrey M. Virges*

# Big Sister Birthday Wishes

I hope you know how much it mean
To have a loving older sister like you,
Who took the time when we were growing up
To help me with my classwork and chores too.

Yesterday is gone, and our paths are far apart
But on you I can still depend,
I love you because you're my big sister
And I also love you as a friend.

I look up to you not because you're older
But because of the love we share,
I am thankful that you're my sister
And because for me you'll always care.
Happy Birthday

Dedicated to my sister
Denise Collins

Audrey M. Virges

# Birthday Joy

This birthday you will cherish forever
Your disposition makes your birthday sweet,
You are surrounded by people you love the most
And there's lots of delicious food to eat.

Because you have made many beautiful memories
We anticipate your birthday with great adoration,
We know you'll cry tears of joy
For this is a joyous celebration.

I know you will be elated over every gift
You are as special as the day is long,
Be thankful today and every day
As we sing your birthday song.

*Audrey M. Virges*

# Happy Birthday Mom

Happy Birthday to our Mom
You really deserve the best,
More than parties, more than money
More than gold in a treasure chest.

Your birthday is a blessing that God allowed you to see
You have been more than a blessing to us,
Your love for us is unselfish and unconditional
Celebrating your birthday is a must.

Enjoy this day; it's your time to shine
We love you more and more each day,
Enjoy this day and live life to its fullest
And celebrate this birthday with cheer.

*Audrey M. Virges*

# Happy Birthday Little One

Happy Birthday to our one year old
While in your high chair you sit,
You don't understand the meaning yet
But we celebrate your birthday with candles lit.

We thank God so much for blessing us with you
You are a blessed armful of joy,
So we celebrate your birthday today
With praise in our heart and bunches of joy.

As you grow and understand the meaning of birthdays
The more excited you will be,
Today we celebrate with joy and laughter
All of our family, your dad and me.

*Audrey M. Virges*

# The Gift of love

Happy Birthday Dad, you're the man of the house
Happy birthday to you,
You are a dad who wears many hats
We're proud of everything you do.

It's hard to choose gifts for you
Because you already have everything,
You give us the gift of love every day
And all the joy you bring.

You have clothes, shoes, tools, and gadgets
And much more than the above,
So I guess we will take you out to dinner
And show you a gift of love.

Audrey M. Virges

# Happy Birthday, Brother

Happy Birthday to you, brother
You're really out of sight,
You can be really aggravating when you want to
But I love you with all my might.

You always got me out of trouble
I consider you my best friend,
No matter how I get on your nerves
On you I can always depend.

I wish you a happy birthday
And I say it very bold,
My hat is off to you this day
You deserve all the best life has to hold.

Audrey M. Virges

# (WEDDING POEMS)

# I Found My Bride

When I found you, I found my bride
And now my search is over,
I want to always be close to you
Like the leaves on a four leaf clover.

I want to spend my life with you
Will you accept my ring?
We can have an everlasting love
And enjoy the happiness that marriage can bring.

I want to spend my life with you
Because there's no one else for me,
I have searched and searched and searched
You are the only one for me.

Audrey M. Virges

# I Married My Best Friend

I am marrying my friend from yesterday
Because we always had so much fun,
We remembered when we laughed and played
In retrospect, I knew you would be the one.

You always listened to what I have to say
And it made me feel so much better,
You became the person I wanted to spend my life with
So we can always be together.

Here we are three weeks before the wedding
I am happier than I have ever been,
We have a loving, joyful, and trusting relationship
Because I am marrying my best friend.

Audrey M. Virges

# Forever Mine

When I met you my whole life changed
And now you're preparing to be my bride,
I love you more than my words can say
I want you forever by my side.

We are about to start a new journey together
Your family's name you will never erase,
My name you will take as long as we live
And no other name will take its place.

We'll be two people sharing our lives together
We have a bond that is tighter than glue,
We'll make this wedding the wedding of a lifetime
Because I'm truly in love with you.

*Audrey M. Virges*

# God Made Us One

When we got married God made us one
When people see you they see me too,
Marriage is the most intimate relationship
I wish the best for me and you.

Marriage isn't always easy
Because we don't always think alike,
Sometimes we reason quite loudly
As if we were talking through a mic.

When we do not agree with each other
We still have to do what's best,
We have to grow in our marriage along the way
And pray God will take care of the rest.

My love you are my soulmate
When we married God made us one,
No matter what differences we have
You are my sweet honey bun.

Audrey M. Virges

# I Will Forever Love You

Today I celebrate my love for you
As your dad walks you up the aisle,
You are arrayed in your beautiful wedding dress
For you I would walk many miles.

When I put the ring on your finger
It's a symbol of my unending love for you,
I knew you would be mine forever
When you looked in my eyes and said I do.

This is the beginning of the rest of our lives
A love that is so special and true,
I promise for the rest of our lives
That I will forever love you.

Audrey M. Virges

# Love Is What It Is

Two hearts that were once in love twenty-one years ago,
Are now reunited again.
Time and distance cannot halt love when love is meant to be;
Now you both stand here in holy matrimony.

Only God knew that at Alcorn's 2008 homecoming
That there you both would meet again.
Love is what it is;
It was all in God's plan.
It's wonderful to have friends
That will help bring joy to your life within,
For the same friend that introduced you to each other
Twenty-one years ago
Assisted in your reuniting again.
Marriage is a sacred institution;
It is ordained by God.
You are to be a help meet to each other
Along this life's journey you trod.
Love is what it is,
Loving and supporting each other in every way.
Love is what it is
Keeping Christ first each and every day.

Love is what it is, Love is what it is

Written exclusively for Dr. Jennifer K. Young
& NFL's Michael Wallace on their wedding day

*Audrey M. Virges*

# We Belong Together

To my sweetheart, my fiancé, my love
I truly pledge my love to you,
You are the only one in the world for me
And I want to live this life's journey with you.

We were once classmates years ago
But we had no interest in each other then,
As we grew up and time passed by
I'm so thankful we met again.

After we met our love kindled
Like a lit lamp with a long wick,
There's one thing I do know
I love you till the mouth of the Mississippi river
Wear lipstick.

I'm grateful we are bonded together
And husband and wife we are about to be,
Now we know we belong to each other
Throughout eternity.

Audrey M. Virges

# Pursuing My Love

When I saw you walk down the street
You were the highlight of my day,
I knew I had to pursue you
I didn't want you to get away.

I was hoping you were not in a relationship
Because I am in search of a wife,
I've been a bachelor for quite some time
I need a companion in my life.

My hope came true and now we're dating
And our love has very well bloomed,
Now I have popped the question
And soon we'll be bride and groom.

In the future we'll live our lives together
In love and wedded bliss we will be,
To share our love for the rest of our lives
In holy matrimony

*Audrey M. Virges*

# (WEDDING ANNIVERSARY POEMS)

# The Love Of Each Other's Life

When we met and fell in love
We became the love of each other's life,
Fifty years ago
God allowed us to become Husband and wife.
Three children God gave us
To share our joy within,
We knew this would be a journey
That we had so proudly begun.
It was our desire to make this life's journey
Right by each other's side,
Our love is as strong as the years were long
In God we did abide.
When our eyes meet and our hands touch
It's just like yesterday,
When we fell in love fifty years ago
Praying we would make it along the way.
A marriage ordained by God_____and_____
Husband and wife, have stood the test of time;
Because we are the love of each other's life.

*Audrey M. Virges*

# 25<sup>th</sup> Wedding Anniversary

On this twenty fifth wedding anniversary
We hold each other's hand
Thinking of the promises we made to each other,
We promised to love and cherish each other forever
And to never seek another.

I grow more and more in love with you each day
I've loved you from the start,
You are the best thing that ever happened to me
And I hope we never be apart.

I thank you so much for the joy you give
And for all the wonderful things you do,
You have made our marriage a comfortable journey
I promise to forever love you.

Audrey M. Virges

# The Rock Of My Life

Happy anniversary to the rock of my life
You are like the shining sun,
Time has gone by like the sands in an hourglass
Our marriage has been quite fun.

How special you have made our life for me
You're my strength when I'm weak,
You managed our home wonderfully
And you are so humble and meek.

I am so thankful for these years
You have always been there for me,
Happy anniversary to the rock of my life
Happy anniversary to you and me.

Audrey M. Virges

# Happy 40ᵗʰ Year Anniversary

Happy 40ᵗʰ year Anniversary to us
And it's because our love still grows,
Our anniversary is a reminder
That we strive as we go.

We do so many things
That is an asset to our lives,
We shop together and we sing together
And we just enjoy being husband and wife.
We enjoyed rearing our children
And our grandchildren God blessed us to see,
We have lived life to its fullest
Trying to be a blessing to others
As much as we can be.

We enjoy seeing each anniversary
As we grow older we will continue to pray,
That our union is always blessed
And many more anniversaries come our way.

Dedicated to Mr. & Mrs. Sam Virges

Audrey M. Virges

# It's The Small Things

Happy anniversary, Honey, we've made it this far
Mostly because of the small things you do,
You have a courteous and well mannered disposition
That really makes you be you.

You don't mind doing small things for me
Like bringing me a glass of water,
And you don't mind pouring my tea,
No matter where we go you always open the door for me.
It takes love and support to keep a marriage together
I know you love me and that's a fact,
After the chores are done and we're all settled in
You take the time to scratch my back.
It doesn't take much to be happy
You have a warm shoulder on which I can lean,
It's wonderful when you come home from work
And bring my favorite ice cream.

It's not the big things that always count
Couples celebrate anniversaries every year,
I count my blessings for the small things,
Let us celebrate this anniversary with cheer.

Audrey M. Virges

# Happy Forty Years

Baby, we've been married forty years
Living each day together,
Through storms, and rain, and sunshine
And through all kinds of weather.

We made lots of plans for our lives
Many of them came through,
Very few couples have been married forty years
That's a plus for me and you.

Each year we love each other more
A great pair we did make,
We loved each other through our illnesses
And with each other we stayed.

Even though we are growing older
We need never to waste precious time,
If we live to see our anniversary next year
I'll still be yours, and you'll still be mine.

Audrey M. Virges

# The Big Sixty

Happy Sixtieth Wedding Anniversary, Sweetheart
I still can say I remember when,
We've lived to see our great grandchildren
And have outlived most of our friends.

Our eyesight is dim, and our steps have gotten short
And we don't get out much any more,
We take care of each other the best we can
And each other we still adore.

The years have taken a toll on us
But our love for each other hasn't changed,
Our looks, our shape, and our bodies
Have gotten somewhat rearranged.

We walk with a cane; It's a good thing to have.
And we walk somewhat with a bend,
We are thankful to see a sixtieth anniversary
Because we'll be together until the end.

*Audrey M. Virges*

# (PASTOR'S ANNIVERSARY POEMS)

# A Pastor's Love

To our pastor and wife on their eight year anniversary
We hold you in our heart so dear,
You both have been a blessing to us in every way
We're so proud God sent you here. These ten
years you have pastored here You have really
shown your love for us, You're here for us when
we're sick, You're here for us when we're sad,
You're here for us when the trials of life weigh us down.
You preach the gospel every Sunday
Hoping someone will be saved
So a new life in Christ they will have found.
You pray for us daily;
You take communion to the sick and shut in,
All your pastoral duties you uphold,
With your wife right by your side, And
with God as your strength
You have many blessings to unfold.
You love each auxiliary
And you want us to do our best
For it's what you do for God that will last
You have many challenges, you have many
tests. So pastor and wife keep doing what you're
doing, Through Christ the battle is fought,
And the victory is won. Keep doing what you're doing
Until God says well done,

Dedicated to Pastor Leroy & First Lady Harriett Bragg

*Audrey M. Virges*

# You Are a Servant

To our pastor and wife of ____ years
_____ Church wants to thank you for your dedicated
And excellent service to us,
And for all the things for our church family you do.

You always tell us that you are a servant
And a servant we know you to be.
You really care for and see after your members
That everyone in our church can see.

You preach hard on Sunday morning
And always teach the word in bible class,
God is with you in whatever you do
No matter the chore or task.

We pray God continues to bless you to lead us
And with humble hearts and minds we'll grow,
May this be a joyous Anniversary for you both
And we'll give God the glory for ever more.

*Audrey M. Virges*

# Our Undershepherd

Happy _____ year Anniversary to our pastor and wife
The undershepherd of _____ Church,
We appreciate you for being our pastor
And we love you very much.

We thank you for keeping us in your prayers
Our church family one and all,
We thank you that when something is wrong
You come very quickly when we call.
We know it takes great love and commitment
To be a watcher over our souls
And you do it to the best of your ability
From the youngest member to the old.

You have a very protective heart
For all your members you truly care,
You feel the hurt from our tribulations
And we are blessed for us you're there.
So pastor, keep being the servant you are
Keep tending the flock God placed in your care,
We know God has His arms around you
Because He knows our burdens you share.

*Audrey M. Virges*

# You're Our Inspiration

To our pastor and wife on
this _____ Pastor's Anniversary
We the _____ Church celebrate you today.
The love of God brought us together
And you both have been a blessing to us in every way.

Your life has been an inspiration to us
Because you live what you preach,
You motivate us to hold to God
Through the inspirational words you preach and teach.

We pray God continue to fill you
With wisdom and knowledge from above,
We also pray you serve here many more years
With the help of God's grace and love.

We salute you for the wonderful work you've rendered
And your words of encouragement you speak so bold,
We love and appreciate you both;
May God smile upon you
And may you receive many blessings to unfold.

Audrey M. Virges

# (THANKSGIVING POEMS)

# Being Thankful

Thanksgiving time is a time to spend with our family
As we celebrate from home to home,
We give thanks for health, family, friends, and food
We're thankful that we're blessed all year long.

We have to be thankful for what we have
Whether we think it's a little or a lot.
If we are thankful when our blessings are few
Then God will send more blessings to you.

Thanksgiving is set aside to express our feelings
And give thanks to God above,
For blessing us all year long
With His magnificent love.

Audrey M. Virges

# Thanksgiving Time

We know it's almost Thanksgiving
When the leaves fall from the trees,
When the harvest is gathered and the hay is baled
And for another year we put up the seeds.

Thanksgiving is a time to be thankful
For the harvest and blessings all year.
Giving thanks is an urgent duty
It adds to Thanksgiving cheer.

There's always something to be thankful for
God has bestowed upon us so many blessings,
Let us enjoy our Thanksgiving holiday
And enjoy our turkey and dressing.

Audrey M. Virges

# Good Thanksgiving Deeds

Thanksgiving time is a wonderful time
A time to do a good deed.
It's a time to share with the less fortunate
And all who are in need.

There are people in homeless shelters
Who unfortunately lost their way,
They're being provided with hot meals
From some church, or organization on Thanksgiving Day.

It's a must to Give God thanks on Thanksgiving
And also to help those in need,
It's a blessing to be able to help others
Because a blessing will return indeed.

Audrey M. Virges

# Thanksgiving Food

Thank God for the turkey
That grace our table so grand,
Thank Him for the green beans
That were snapped by Mom's hands.

Thank God for the yams
That were dug from the ground,
Peeled, cut and seasoned
And put in the oven forty minutes down.

Thank God for the dressing
That was made from the bread,
That was made from the cornmeal
From the barrel in the shed.

Thank God for the corn
That was cut off the cob,
That specked up our glasses
Oh!! What a job.

Thank God for the potatoes
That were dug from the earth,
Laid on a pallet, washed, peeled,
And cut up and cooked

To make a delicious potato salad.
Thank God for the greens
That were picked from the ground,
Washed about four times around,
Put in a pot, seasoned with meat,
And put it on the table for all to eat.

*Audrey M. Virges*

# Thanksgiving Family Time

Thanksgiving is a time for family and friends
To share in what each other does. It's a
time to prepare a special meal
And to thank God for blessing us too.

On Thanksgiving morning the Rose Bowl parade is
showing, and we see the different marching bands.
We also see the beautifully decorated floats
With cartoon characters waving their hands.

After the Thanksgiving meal is over,
And the family visits are done, guess what?
The football game begins
Everyone is cheering their team on
Hoping that their team wins.

These are some of the things at Thanksgiving
That God allows us to enjoy,
Everyday is a day of thanksgiving
That we should be thankful for.

*Audrey M. Virges*

# A Blessed Day

Thanksgiving is a blessed day
To be with family and eat our fill,
It's a time to fellowship with our relatives
Who came to share in our meal.

We play games with our relatives
And look at photo albums from years ago,
We are thankful to see Thanksgiving year after year
We are so very blessed we know.

Audrey M. Virges

# (CHRISTMAS POEMS)

# Journey to Bethlehem

Mary rode the donkey to Bethlehem
While Joseph walked by her side,
Mary expecting to soon deliver baby Jesus
The journey wasn't a comfortable ride.

When they arrived at Bethlehem
There were no rooms in the Inn,
Every home was crowded.
Even no room with the next of kin.

They were proud to find room in a manger
Mary was so tired and worn,
It was there where she gave birth to our Savior
On that blessed Christmas morning.

Audrey M. Virges

# Singing At Christmas Time

We sing Christmas carols
As we stroll from door to door
Telling about our baby Jesus's birth,
We walk through every street in town
Telling that King Jesus would rule the earth.

We sing the song, "Silent Night Holy Night"
At each doorbell we ring,
We sing the song, "Joy To The World"
Let earth receive her king.

We sing the song," Away In A Manger"
Because asleep on the hay was the little Jesus child,
We sing, "Jesus What A wonderful Child"
Because He was so meek and mild.

We enjoy singing Christmas carols at Christmas
And we are excited about each doorbell we
ring, We love letting everyone know
That Jesus is surely the King.

*Audrey M. Virges*

# The Spirit of Christmas

I love the spirit of Christmas
I wish it lasts all year through the year,
It's the spirit of love and giving
That brings joy and cheer.

People are shopping from store to store
Buying gifts for family and friends,
Others are restoring relationships
Trying to make amends.

Salvation Army bells are ringing
Hoping to receive lots of giving,
When people reach out and help the less fortunate
That's the real spirit of living.

Don't be disappointed if you don't receive a gift
As long as a gift you can give,
When you learn to show love and compassion
Is when you really begin to live.

*Audrey M. Virges*

# Our Children at Christmas

I awake on Christmas morning
Thankful to see the day,
I'm excited to see our children's reaction
As they open their gifts and play.

The train set is ready to roll
The Bigwheel is ready to ride,
They really enjoy their viewmaster
As they chick it from slide to slide.

The necklace set is full of jewels
And it is ready to wear,
The Barbie doll is beautifully dressed
And our daughter can comb her hair.

I love watching our children play at Christmas
They have toys to ride and race,
But most of all I love to see
Their precious little happy faces.

Audrey M. Virges

# Make Someone Happy at Christmas

Christmas is a joyous time
But for some it can be sad,
Jesus is the reason for the season
That should make everyone glad.

We pinch our pennies and save our dimes
For we know Christmas is on the way,
We should have the spirit of Christmas
Each and every day.

If you have little cash to spend
And you cannot buy Christmas gifts,
Give your gift of time and help someone in need.
It doesn't take much to make someone happy
Just showing a little love will make them have
A merry Christmas indeed.

Audrey M. Virges

# Grandma's House at Christmas

At Grandma's house at Christmas
Is sweet food everywhere.
She has sweets in the kitchen, sweets in the dining room
And even sweets up stairs.

She makes big white coconut cakes
With the icing light and fluffy,
She make small fruit cakes
With nuts and fruit tight and stuffy.

She make egg pies golden brown
When she cut a slice it is wiggly,
She make a strawberry jello mold
When she shakes it, it is jiggly.

She make peanut brittle so crunchy
And candies made in every way.
This is the way we know Grandma's house
On every Christmas day.

Audrey M. Virges

# Jesus Was Born

Jesus was born on Christmas Day
In such a lowly birth,
He brought love, joy, and happiness
As well as peace on earth.

*Audrey M. Virges*

# Jesus Lives

I see Christmas lights and Christmas trees
And presents on the floor.
It let's me know Christ's birthday is near
And He'll live forever more.

Audrey M. Virges

# Giving Gifts

We give gifts at Christmas
And that is very nice,
But what is really great
Is giving our heart to Christ.

Audrey M. Virges

# A Holy Night

It was a holy night when Jesus was born
By a star the wise men were led,
They found baby Jesus asleep
In a trough full of hay for a bed.

Audrey M. Virges

# The Greatest Gift

Hang the lights and trim your tree
And Oh!!! Just deck the halls,
Jesus is our Savior,
The greatest gift of all.

*Audrey M. Virges*

# Jesus Is Love

The wise men followed the star
And found Jesus who is love,
We must follow Jesus
To live with God above.

Audrey M. Virges

# Jesus In Me

When I awake on Christmas morning
Gifts I do expect to see,
But I smile when I know
That you see Jesus In me.

*Audrey M. Virges*

# Staying up Late

We are waiting up on Christmas Eve
Not wanting to go to bed,
We stay up as long as possible
Waiting to hear Santa's sled.

Mom is baking cookies
For Santa when he bring the toys,
At last we fell asleep
So we wouldn't make any noise.

We awake Christmas morning
To find presents under the tree,
We are very, very, happy
As happy as can be.

Audrey M. Virges

# A Snowy Christmas Day

Christmas really seem like Christmas
When there's snow on the ground,
You can take gifts from house to house
Making footprints all through town.

It's a wonderful winter day
The air is cold, and the snow is bright,
The Christmas lights glow through the snow,
And they look so beautiful at night.

Some people dream of a white Christmas
Wishing to see the snowflakes fall,
Some of their dreams come true and they see
The most beautiful Christmas of all.

Audrey M. Virges

# (OTHER POEMS OF INSPIRATION)

# Believe In Yourself

If you don't believe in yourself
Who will?
You have to believe in yourself
Then your dreams you'll fulfill.

Believe you can make it
Although life will be a ride,
The challenges of life can be disappointing
In God you must abide.

Believe in yourself that you can be
Whatever you want to be,
Make an effort in that direction.
Strive hard to reach that point
And soon you'll reach perfection.

Audrey M. Virges

# Love

Love is the greatest gift of the spirit
It is an intense feeling of deep affection,
If you have love one for another
You know you're on the right direction.
You have to show love your whole life through
And believe that love you will receive,
The same act of affection that you give
Will come back around just you believe.
Love is the glue that holds families together
Without it relationships cannot thrive,
Where there is no love there's no unity
When developing relationships you must be wise.
Love won't let you hold a grudge
When someone has done you wrong,
Love allows you to forgive
So relationships can roll right along.
Love is a necessity because God is love
We must have love and compassion to give,
God is love and the source of life
You must have love to live.

Audrey M. Virges

# It's your Choice

You choose your own attitude
You don't have to lose your cool,
It's good to practice self control
That's a very important tool.

You can get irritated with someone
Who got up on the wrong side of the bed,
It's your choice to handle the situation
Whereas not to cause headaches to your head.

You have to learn how to pray for that person
And not let their bad mood change you,
You stay calm, cool, and collected.
That's the best thing to do.

*Audrey M. Virges*

# A Smile

A smile is a beautiful thing
And it really means so much,
It can cause people to make friends easier
Who will want to keep in touch.

A smile doesn't cost a thing
It'll lift someone's spirit who's having a bad day,
Everyone responds better to a smiling face
And honors them in a trustworthy way.

So keep a smile on your face
No matter what mood you're in,
The same people who saw you before
Will enjoy seeing you again.

*Audrey M. Virges*

# A Real Friend

Friends won't talk about you behind your back
They'll do it in front of your face.
No one can tell you something they said
There will be nothing to erase.
Friends will critique you
In such a humble way,
That you will appreciate them and be thankful
That they care for you each day.
A friend will stick with you
And that is truly a fact,
A fake friend will say I got you
And it will really be way back. Friends
check up on you from time to time
To see if you are O'K,
They talk to you and encourage you
When you're having a bad day.
You have close relatives, and coworkers
And certainly next of kin, But you have a great
asset When you have a true friend.

*Audrey M. Virges*

# Life Is A Challenge

The harder the challenge
The more you grow,
Challenges make you stronger
The more you learn, the more you grow.

When practicing for a spelling bee
Harder the words you will have to learn,
They get harder to spell each time,
Persistent study is the challenge,
But you'll be at the top of your line.

It's a challenge to lose twenty lbs. a month
And not eat the food you like,
It's more of a challenge to exercise
Whether it's walking or riding a bike.

Anything is a challenge that you have to work towards
It's not easy, but it can be done,
Buckle up, and believe you can
And try to make each challenge fun.

Audrey M. Virges

# Karma

Karma is something we all will experience
The bible say we reap what we sow,
We all have sinned and come short of God's glory
That we all should know.

It's best to live our best for God
And treat ourselves and our fellow man right,
Karma is a good whipping
With either more or less stripes.

Some people don't think much about it
And some it make a little tense,
But if we don't get it in the washing
We'll get it in the rinse.

Audrey M. Virges

# A Helping Hand

Sometimes it's a heartfelt duty
To lend a helping hand,
It's not only good to help family
But it's good to help our fellow man.

Life is about love and serving others
It's about putting others first,
It's good to be concerned about others
An act of kindness means so much.

So take an interest and do a good deed
And help make someone's day
The same help that you give to someone
You just might need one day.

Audrey M. Virges

# Don't Worry

Worrying doesn't solve anything
It only makes it worse,
You can worry too much
And you will have to visit the doctor or nurse.

You can worry too much
And it will disrupt your sleep,
You know it's too much
When it causes you to weep.

You can worry too much
That your body will get out of whack,
Adding more worry to your brain
Might give you a heart attack.

You see worry doesn't solve anything
It's really caused by fear,
Pray to God for the answer
And save yourself some tears.

Audrey M. Virges

# Storms of Life

We all go through storms of life
And we know forever they will not last,
So hold on and stay in constant prayer
That the storm will soon pass.

People go through storms different
Some go through with doubt,
Some go through storms with the spirit of hope
That God will soon bring them out.

The storms of life can be rough
The night is always darkest before the dawn,
Be humble and pray that God will change things
Before you get all battered and worn.

*Audrey M. Virges*

# A Home

Home is a place we should look forward to going
After a long day of work or just being away.
It is a place of love and comfort
To look forward to each day.

A home is where a family lives
No matter where it is or in what direction,
It is decorated with beautiful things a family likes
And it is filled with love and affection.

In a home each member is loved
It's a place we can call our own,
We can visit anybody or any place in the world
But there's nothing like going back home.

Audrey M. Virges

# Love Your Job

People go through life
Experiencing having to work every day,
But if you're blessed with a job you love
It makes it easier in every way.

If you love your job
You will be dedicated in what you do,
You'll make less mistakes
Which will be beneficial to you.

Work for the moment
And don't worry about the next chore,
Loving your job takes the work out of it
So you'll enjoy your job even more.

Doing what you love
Doesn't mean it'll be sunshine every day,
But it'll make life a little easier
And more pleasant will be your pay.

Audrey M. Virges

# Success

Some say success is many different things
Some say it's their education,
Some say it's a big house on a hill,
Some say it's having furrs and diamond rings
And all these are fine for real.

Success is also being happy in life
And being happy with what you do,
Success is bringing out the best in others
And having a good vision, too.

Success is living a satisfying life
And living your best for the Lord,
It's being in fellowship with your fellow man
And being on one accord.

Success is not throwing in the towel
When life is not treating you right,
It's hanging in there and never giving up
And staying in the fight.

Audrey M. Virges

MRS. VIRGES poetry is written very unique. The reader will be interested in her voice as a writer because her poetry is so personal and heartfelt. They hold the reader's interest. She feels what she writes and she writes so the meaning of her poetry is clearly understood. Mrs. Virges writes knowing that the reader will receive comfort, inspiration and encouragement.

Contact me at audreyvirges@yahoo.com

Printed in the United States
By Bookmasters